A Book of Remembrances

Diana
Princess of Wales

1961-1997

A Book of Remembrances

Diana
Princess of Wales
1961-1997

COURAGE
BOOKS
AN IMPRINT OF RUNNING PRESS
PHILADELPHIA • LONDON

Unattributed quotations in this book have been selected
from the tens of thousands of personal tributes addressed to
Diana by members of the public – part of the spontaneous
wave of grief and affection for her that swept the world
following the news of her death.

5090 Diana: A Book of Remembrances
Published in 1997 for Courage Books, an imprint of
Running Press Book Publishers
125 South Twenty-second Street
Philadelphia, Pennsylvania 19103-4399

© 1997 CLB International, a division of Quadrillion Publishing Ltd,
Godalming, England GU7 1XW
All rights reserved
ISBN 0-7624-0355-1
Printed in the USA

Library of Congress Cataloging-in-Publication Number 97-77152

Designed, produced and packaged by Stonecastle Graphics Ltd
Tonbridge, England TN12 9LS

Compiled by Paul Turner and Sue Pressley
Introductory text by Lesley Bellew
Picture research by Brooks Krikler Research

The publishers would like to thank the following picture libraries
who have supplied photographs for this book:
Rex Features London
Frank Spooner Pictures/Gamma Presse Images
PA News Photo Library
Mirror Syndication International
Photofusion
Additional photography by Neil Sutherland

Front cover photograph:
Camera Press London/Snowdon

Queen of Hearts

Everyone will always remember exactly where they were on the day when they heard the tragic news of Princess Diana's death. In 36 short years she had captured the hearts of millions throughout the world. They were captivated by her natural beauty, her compassion, her dedicated work for charity and her vulnerability. The world was truly lit up by her kindness. Her life was a fairytale that turned into a nightmare for us all.

Never has there been such a national display of public grief and we all have our reasons for proclaiming her the nation's Queen of Hearts. Here we record those days of mourning and the final farewell from the people she loved, and who loved her.

This special book gives you a chance to note your own private memories and fondest thoughts, and to add your favourite photographs and press cuttings to compile your family's personal book of remembrance.

6 September 1997

Mankind is many rivers
That only want to run.
Holy Tragedy and Loss
Make the many One.
Mankind is a Holy, crowned
Mother and her Son.
For worship, for mourning:
God is here, is gone.
Love is broken on the Cross.
The Flower on the Gun.

TED HUGHES,
POET LAUREATE

The Making of a Princess

Diana had an early introduction to royal life. She was born and brought up on the royal estate at Sandringham, Norfolk, where her father was an equerry to The Queen. But it was at the end of 1980 that Diana first walked into the heart of the nation as the blushing 19-year-old in the company of Prince Charles. The fairytale romance led to their marriage in July 1981. The world was caught up in wedding fever; one billion people tuned into television and radio to witness the ceremony.

Diana quickly enchanted the nation with her beauty and her captivating smile. She won even more hearts when, in June 1982, she gave birth to a son and heir to the throne, William. Motherhood made her blossom and her second son Harry was born in September 1984. Her boys meant everything to her and it was her natural compassion and love as a mother which radiated through her charity work.

I never told you,
It was not my place,
To say how much I loved you.
Though we never met,
I mourn, as many millions will,
The dying of your light,
Which shone and sparkled in
the dark,
Of so many blighted and
unhappy lives.

Your world was so different from
what we knew,
We ordinary people with such
humdrum lives.
Yours sparkled, roller-coasted,
high and low,
In blinding light that we created,
And yet you were the same as us.

. . . the unique, the complex, the extraordinary
and irreplaceable Diana . . .

THE EARL SPENCER

My memories of the wedding

_____

_____

_____

_____

_____

They're two lovely
boys and Britain
should remember how
Diana brought them
up with love.

Our thoughts and prayers
to Prince William, Harry
and family. Where we all are
now, Diana once was, and
where Diana is now, we all
shall be.

⁓

This wonderful woman was
a jewel in the crown of
England and will never be
replaced. She will be so
sadly missed.

I felt so much for Diana. I admired her so much for her work with children and people with AIDS.

She was thrust into the limelight
At a very early age,
She never could have realised
The commitment at this stage.

But she entered it and did
her best
In her shy retiring way,
Gaining strength and confidence
A little more each day.
With her beauty and compassion
She hypnotised the world,
And proved a great ambassador
As the years unfurled.

She had a way of touching
And getting through to Man,
The deprived, the sick, the lonely
Could relate to our Diana.

No matter where this Lady went,
Any distant land,
She seemed to make things better
Just by reaching out her hand.

Little children loved her,
She'd put them on her knee.
Sickness never bothered her,
The whole wide world could see.

Now the world has lost her
Our Princess has now gone,
But her smile will live forever
And her good work will go on.

Her children will be proud of her,
There'll never be another,
Like the one who changed so
many things,
The one that they called Mother.

A Tragic Dawn

$\mathcal{A}$s the nation woke to the shocking news on Sunday, 31 August, 1997 that Diana, Princess of Wales was dead, it seemed unbelievable. An impossible nightmare. News bulletins that she and her companion, Dodi Fayed, had perished in a late-night car crash in Paris were too horrendous to take in.

While the country wept for a terrible waste of life, the Prince of Wales and Diana's sisters, Lady Sarah McCorquodale and Lady Jane Fellowes, flew to France to bring home her body encased in a simple casket draped in the Royal Standard.

She was gently lifted from the BAe 146 which had flown her across the Channel to RAF Northolt. Here a bitter wind swept the airfield as her coffin was carried to a waiting hearse ready to take her to the Royal Chapel at St James's Palace. The woman who, with a touch, a smile or a kiss could inspire others, was gone.

Through the death of Diana I feel that many people will realise the fragility of life. I have been touched by the caring and understanding she had of others.

What a wonderful place the world would be if we all tried to follow Princess Diana's example in some small way.

The world has lost a saint and heaven has gained the most beautiful angel that God has ever created.

No earthly prince can wake her, now it's our turn to cry, carelessly we slept whilst her graceful spirit soared, arrow straight, into a most glorious morning sky.

My feelings when I heard that
Princess Diana had died

*One thing we know
for sure,
Now she's gone we'll miss
her more,
And now she rests with
God above,
Our Princess,
whom we killed with love.
Diana, Queen of
our hearts
Deeply loved, sadly missed.*

In fond memory of Princess Diana, whose warmth, beauty and compassion shone like a beacon throughout the world, and her lover Dodi, who had given her so much happiness, and had shown her so much kindness and understanding.

People flocked to add their personal tributes to the growing piles of flowers at the gates of Buckingham Palace (above far left) and Kensington Palace (above left and above).

I feel like everyone else in this country today – utterly devastated. Our thoughts and prayers are with Princess Diana's family – in particular her two sons. Our hearts go out to them. We are today a nation in a state of shock, in mourning, in grief that is so deeply painful for us.

She was a wonderful and warm human being. Though her own life was often sadly touched by tragedy, she touched the lives of so many others in Britain – throughout the world – with joy and with comfort. How many times shall we remember her, in how many different ways? With the sick, the dying, with children, with the needy – when, with just a look or a gesture that spoke so much more than words, she would reveal to all of us the depth of her compassion and her humanity.

How difficult things were for her from time to time, surely we can only guess at – but the people everywhere, not just here in Britain, but everywhere, they kept faith with Princess Diana, they liked her, they loved her, they regarded her as one of the people. She was the People's Princess. That's how she will stay, how she will remain in our hearts forever.

She seemed full of happiness, full of life, she was great fun to be with and she was an unusual but a really warm character and personality.

I will remember her personally with very great affection. I think the whole country will remember her with the deepest affection and love – and that is why our grief is so deep today.

TONY BLAIR, PRIME MINISTER

I hold you close within my heart
and there you shall remain,
To walk with me throughout
my life
until we meet again.
So rest in peace dear one,
and thanks for all you've done.
I pray that God has given you
the crown you truly won.

Since last Sunday's dreadful news, we have seen throughout Britain and around the world an overwhelming expression of sadness at Diana's death.

We have all been trying in our own different ways to cope. It is not easy to express a sense of loss, since the initial shock is often succeeded by a mixture of other feelings — disbelief, incomprehension, anger and concern for those who remain.

We have all felt those emotions in these last few days. So what I say to you now, as your Queen and as a grandmother, I say from my heart.

First, I want to pay tribute to Diana myself. She was an exceptional and gifted human being. In good times and bad, she never lost her capacity to smile and laugh, nor to inspire others with her warmth and kindness.

I admired and respected her — for her energy and commitment to others, and especially for her devotion to her two boys.

This week at Balmoral, we have all been trying to help William and Harry come to terms with the devastating loss that they and the rest of us have suffered.

No one who knew Diana will ever forget her. Millions of others who never met her, but felt they knew her, will remember her.

I, for one, believe that there are lessons to be drawn from her life and from the extraordinary and moving reaction to her death.

I share in your determination to cherish her memory. This is also an opportunity for me, on behalf of my family and especially Prince Charles and William and Harry, to thank all of you who have brought flowers, sent messages and paid your respects in so many ways to a remarkable person.

These acts of kindness have been a huge source of help and comfort.

Our thoughts are also with Diana's family and the families of those who died with her. I know that they too have drawn strength from what has happened since last weekend, as they seek to heal their sorrow and then to face the future without a loved one.

I hope that tomorrow we can all, wherever we are, join in expressing our grief at Diana's loss and gratitude for her all-too-short life.

It is a chance to show to the whole world the British nation united in grief and respect.

May those who died rest in peace and may we, each and every one of us, thank God for someone who made many, many people happy.

HER MAJESTY THE QUEEN

The People's Princess

A grieving nation swamped by an ocean of tears paid tribute to Diana in an unprecedented wave of emotion. In their thousands they came to lay flowers and leave heartfelt messages at the gates of Kensington Palace, Buckingham Palace and even in the street outside Harrods, the famous store owned by Mohamed Al Fayed, the father of Diana's companion, Dodi.

The people were drawn by a deep affection and need to express their sorrow. Some knelt at the growing bank of flowers and wept; others stood silently lost in their thoughts and memories. Mourners lit candles on the pavement in front of Kensington Palace, which became a shrine to Diana.

Books of Condolence were opened at St James's Palace and queues of people waited through the night to pen their personal message to the Princess they had taken to their hearts. The demand was so great that more and more books had to be provided.

I always thought to write to you,
Diana, kind and good,
You always seemed so lonely,
But I never felt I could.

I watched your eyes so closely,
Sometimes they showed despair
Amidst a sea of faces,
Few friends to show they care.

Your courage was remarkable,
You almost conquered all,
But lost into the darkness
That fatal last Press call.

Lost moments, years, a lifetime,
The world will love you, still —
I would have loved to talk to you
And now I never will.

A pure English rose,
Lent not given,
To bud on earth,
Then bloom in Heaven,
God Bless.

She was our hero, she was
the wind beneath our wings,
and she was what women
everywhere would like to be.
She will be sadly missed,
an inspiration.

*In this season she was born
to bloom,
This summer rose was taken.
To heaven sped her
summer soul,
There to re-awaken.
Now this child will find
her peace,
And Godly comfort take.
Among the angels she
will sparkle
And thus an angel make.*

A star will shine in the
midnight sky,
And all of us would have
said goodbye,
But one little star will
twinkle from above,
Which will be you Diana
looking down with love.

You are a rose that
has perished in such a
harsh and dry
environment. I hope
that your seed of love
and tenderness
blossoms through
your dear children.

You had a sadness that made you strong, the world is sad that you have gone. You were how we should be – loving, caring, comforting, embracing all. Now in death, Princess of Love, you touch our hearts with undying love.

As we shed so many tears for you, our Queen of Hearts, the sparkling light you became has now gone out. You were the most regal royal that we have ever known and yet you were one of us, here and around the world.

❧

The void you have left cannot be filled. No one can take your place. And we will always remember you as simply the best.

What a shame fairytales have to end. We'll always remember your smile, efforts and how you made our ugly world so much brighter.

Too great a loss!
Too soon,
Too great a gift to lose.
Sweet Princess.

A beautiful face and heart
of gold,
With arms stretched out to touch
and hold,
An English rose that bloomed
so fair,
Who showed the world the way
to care,
A lady full of style and grace,
Now Heaven is a richer place.

In life, she was an angel among princesses.
Now, she is a princess among angels.
God has blessed her.

A withered rose,
An autumn tree,
A gentle breeze . . .
Gone too soon.

A silent prayer,
A heartfelt wish,
A helping hand . . .
Gone too soon.

A burning light,
An open book,
A guiding star . . .
Gone too soon.

A magic touch,
A lively soul,
An unfinished fairy-tale . . .
Gone too soon.

There are words for
every occasion,
Whether they be good, or bad.
There are words that make
you happy,
And words that make you sad.
But right now, no amount
of words,
Could ever be enough.
So I'd just like to say,
Diana, thanks, simply for
being one of us.

To live in the hearts
of those you leave
behind is not to die.

It feels that the Great has now gone out of Britain although the majority of us are united in our grief.

She was like the seasons. When she came on the scene she was like a flower waiting to bloom.

We all witnessed her beauty in the summer of her life. Now autumn has come and she's gone away. Winter will be empty without her. But in William and Harry, spring will come again.

I am standing on the seashore. A ship in the bay lifts her anchor, spreads her white sails to the morning's breeze and starts out upon the ocean. She is an object of beauty and strength and I stand and watch her until she hangs like a speck of white cloud, just where the sea and sky mingle with each other.

Then someone at my side says: 'There, she's gone.' Gone where? Gone from view, that is all. Just at that moment, there are other eyes watching her coming and other souls taking up the glad shout: 'There, she's coming.'
And that is dying.

Reaching out and holding
hands, doing things that
she believed.

Her charity work meant the
world to her, so much that
she risked her life.

Towards the end she found
happiness. She deserved it.
Diana was the People's
Princess as well as the
Queen of Hearts.

To me she is still alive, alive
in my heart.

My own message to Princess Diana

You lit up our lives with your radiant smile, each one of us felt your warmth and loving kindness.

As we mourn for your sad loss of life, it seems that the light has gone out, and darkness is everywhere.

But your light will not be extinguished, you will continue to shine in everyone's heart.

You touched so many hearts and lives with just a smile or a touch, that although you may be gone, you will never be forgotten. Rest in peace my bright angel, stay beautiful forever.

The angels wept in Heaven
On the day Diana died,
They opened up their loving arms
And held her safe inside.

No more will people sadden her,
With rumours or with lies,
For she has prematurely gone
To a haven in the skies.

In cities, towns and villages around Britain, in churches, cathedrals and on village greens, ordinary people paid their last respects to Princess Diana with floral tributes and messages of heartfelt sympathy at her death.

God kissed your brow when you were born
And painted your hand gold,
And sent you out into this land
To warm a world so cold.
Your beauty charmed each one you met,
Your touch healed those in pain,
And though we hurt in our sad loss
Your death is not in vain.
You've brought the world together
And joined a billion hearts,
To the broken jigsaw of our lives you've linked a million parts.
Once upon a time God sent
A son to teach us love,
Now God's reclaimed His daughter
And taken her above.

Sleep well, our beloved princess.

The break of day's upon us,
But darkness still prevails,
The earth itself is weeping,
At the death of the Princess
of Wales.

The sound of voices praying,
Their voices racked with pain,
A nation shedding tears,
A public show of pain.

When at last the light
breaks through,
And we can see more clearly,
In death, as in life itself,
This country loves you dearly.

So climb those stairs and take
your place,
An angel in her rightful place.
As you take your seat above,
You take with you this
country's love.

To me Princess Diana was a loving, caring person who reached out to each and every one of us by being one of us. Her beauty, which shone from deep within her, outshone that of the most beautiful supermodels.

She gave dignity to our society, she touched the untouchable, she reached the unreachable, she gave hope to the hopeless, she really was our Queen of Hearts.

You did so much in little time,
You've opened so many doors,
I must admit my life on earth
Is nothing compared with yours.

God has made a big mistake
By taking you away,
There's no one else to take
your place,
He should have let you stay.

You helped so many people,
You've changed their lives for good,
You listened to their problems
And you always understood.

If anyone could change places
with you I'm sure there'd be
no hesitation,
You were known throughout
the world,
You were loved by every nation.

God must have had His reasons
For taking you above,
But one thing He cannot take
Is our love for Diana, our love.

Goodnight sweet
beautiful angel, may you
rest in peace.

You were a beautiful,
caring and very
special person.

Diana was the People's Princess, not just in Scotland, England, Ireland and Wales but the world over.

She transcended race, age, colour, class and religion. Our loss is both personal and universal.

Born to be a Princess, you were
our future Queen,
But this was changed to memories
of how things might have been,
The light has gone from
many hearts,
You had that magic touch,
You radiated kindness, we loved
you very much,
You leave behind a legacy, your
sons will take your place,
I pray Dear Lord they have
your heart.
You were our saving grace.

The World Mourns

She was the world's most famous face – the woman who entranced millions around the globe. She was the only woman on this planet who could dance with John Travolta at the White House and yet be equally at ease ministering to the sick with Mother Teresa. World figures not only expressed their personal sadness but poured out praise for her dedication and humanity.

The rich and famous had become personal friends and admirers of this charismatic ambassador of worthy causes and, indeed, Great Britain. But it was not just the great names who flocked to pay tribute to Diana. Candles were lit and flowers laid around the world. Wherever she went, she had the extraordinary gift of being able to reach out and touch people physically, spiritually and emotionally. Armed with nothing more potent than a smile and a warm embrace, she gave more pleasure and affection than anyone else in the world.

Princess Diana will be sadly missed as a warm, compassionate and caring person. I was tremendously impressed by her. She was undoubtedly one of the best ambassadors of Great Britain. She was highly intelligent and committed to worthy causes. She became an ambassador for landmine victims, war orphans and the world's sick and needy.

NELSON MANDELA

A bright light has been extinguished. The world is a darker place, a much darker place.

OPRAH WINFREY

She was in love with the
poor, anxious to do
something for them. That
is why we were so close.
All the sisters and I are
praying for her and all the
members of her family to
know God's speed and
peace and comfort in
this moment.

MOTHER TERESA

(Just five days later the Nobel-
prize-winning nun, who had
dedicated her life to caring for
the destitute and dying,
died at the age of 87.)

The Princess was
well known and loved
by the Russian people.

**BORIS YELTSIN,
RUSSIAN PRESIDENT**

Many people in Germany
loved her because of her
openness and humanitarian
engagement.

**HELMUT KOHL, GERMAN
CHANCELLOR**

Hillary and I knew Princess Diana and we were very fond of her. We are profoundly saddened by this tragic event. We liked her very much. We admired her for her work for children, for people with AIDS, for the cause of ending the scourge of landmines in the world and for her love for her children, William and Harry.

I know this is a very difficult time for millions in the United Kingdom, who are deeply shocked and grieving, and the American people send their condolences to all of them.

BILL CLINTON, US PRESIDENT

It was profoundly sad that this beautiful young woman, loved by the people, and whose every act and gesture was scrutinised, should end her life tragically in France, in Paris.

LIONEL JOSPIN, FRENCH PREMIER PRIME MINISTER

In New York (above), Los Angeles (left), and throughout America, many people mourned the death of Princess Diana in spontaneous displays of grief.

The death, in such tragic circumstances, has ended at a young age the life of a person who held a particular fascination for many people around the world.

JOHN HOWARD, AUSTRALIAN PRIME MINISTER

The Princess was a woman of grace, beauty and charm. She represented Britain with nobility and warmth, and she captured the imagination of millions throughout the world.

BINYAMIN NETANYAHU, ISRAELI PRIME MINISTER

My heart is full of grief and pain. Princess Diana was the most beautiful symbol of humanity and love for all the world.

She touched my life in an extraordinary way. I'll always remember her with deep love and joy.

LUCIANO PAVAROTTI

When I first heard the news I cried a lot, and for many reasons. I don't like the idea of a meaningful life cut short, and I cry for her children. It's hard for me to imagine what it will do to them. Oh, how I'll miss her.

JOHN TRAVOLTA

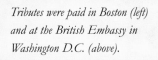

Tributes were paid in Boston (left) and at the British Embassy in Washington D.C. (above).

I feel so sorry for the whole family, but especially those boys. What a horrible, horrible tragedy. God help us all.

ELIZABETH TAYLOR

The tragedy has robbed the world of a consistent and committed voice for the improvement of the lives of suffering children worldwide.

KOFI ANNAN, UN SECRETARY-GENERAL

Diana's Funeral

Silently, millions of people lined the streets of London as Diana's coffin was carried on a gun carriage down The Mall, through Horse Guards and along Whitehall to Westminster Abbey. Millions more watched their television sets in Britain and around the world to view the sombre procession. The Queen bowed her head as the carriage passed Buckingham Palace. For the first time in history the Union Flag was flown at half-mast above the Palace. But it was to Diana's beloved sons that the world reached out as they filed behind the coffin with The Prince of Wales, Prince Philip and Earl Spencer. Poignantly, they were followed by representatives of Diana's 100 favourite charities.

It was this blend of tradition and modernity that was to characterise the funeral service. It had been carefully planned to encompass hymns and music so very special to her. As her coffin emerged from the Abbey, the hands of Big Ben crept to 12.05pm and the nation was shrouded in silence. For one minute, young and old honoured their Princess. Rarely had a mark of respect been so widely observed throughout the country.

Westminster Abbey

FUNERAL OF DIANA PRINCESS OF WALES

Saturday 6 September 1997
11.00 a.m.

We heard the hooves of the horses pulling the gun carriage in the distance. Everyone fell silent.

The coffin started to pass by me and I was surprised at how small it looked – dwarfed by the soldiers and horses. A woman nearby started screaming hysterically as did several others. It was a horrible sound – like raw grief.

I was sobbing too, tears running down my face and my mother was weeping uncontrollably.

I wanted someone to grab me and say it was not true.

What a waste. Our Prayers are
with you and your lovely sons.

During the Procession of the Cortege from Kensington Palace, the Tenor Bell is tolled every minute.

The service is sung by the Choir of Westminster Abbey, conducted by Martin Neary, Organist and Master of the Choristers.
The organ is played by Martin Baker, Sub-Organist of Westminster Abbey.

Music before the service, played by Stephen Le Prevost, Assistant Organist, Westminster Abbey:

Second Movement (Grave),
Organ Sonata, no. 2
Felix Mendelssohn-Bartholdy (1809-47)

Prelude on the hymn tune *'Eventide'*
Hubert Parry (1848-1918)

Adagio in E
Frank Bridge (1879-1941)

Prelude on the hymn tune *'Rhosymedre'*
Ralph Vaughan Williams (1872-1958)

Choral prelude: *Ich ruf' zu dir, Herr Jesu Christ,*
BWV639
Johann Sebastian Bach (1685-1750)

Elegy
George Thalben-Ball (1896-1988)

Martin Baker plays:

Fantasia in C minor, BWV537
Johann Sebastian Bach

Adagio in G Minor
Tomaso Giovanni Albinoni (1671-1751)

Slow movement, from the Ninth Symphony
(*'From The New World'*)
Antonin Dvorak (1841-1904)

Canon
Johann Pachelbel (1653-1706)

Nimrod, Variation 9 arranged from Variations on an Original Theme (*Enigma*) Op.36
Edward Elgar (1857-1934)

Prelude
William Harris (1883-1973)

The Members of the Spencer Family are received at the Great West Door by the Dean and Chapter of Westminster.
All stand as they are conducted to places in the North Lantern, and then sit.

All stand as the Procession of Visiting Clergy moves to places in the Sacrarium, and then sit.

Members of the Royal Family are received at the Great West Door by the Dean and Chapter of Westminster and are conducted to St George's Chapel.

All stand as they are conducted to places in the South Lantern, and then sit.
Her Majesty The Queen,
Her Majesty Queen Elizabeth The Queen Mother, and His Royal Highness The Prince Philip, Duke of Edinburgh, are received at the Great West Door by the Dean and Chapter of Westminster.

All stand as Their Majesties and His Royal Highness are conducted to their places in the South Lantern.

Today is a day of memories of the Princess — and the emblem of that memory should be a bright light.

The first thing I noticed was the silence. It almost swept over us as the coffin approached.
A few people clapped. Some threw flowers.

Then, almost as soon as it was here, it was gone again. . . and that was it.

I still can't believe she has gone. She was such a beautiful and colourful Princess.

Where I was on the day of Diana's Funeral

_____

_____

_____

_____

_____

All remain standing as the Cortege enters the Great West Door.

The Collegiate Body of St Peter in Westminster moves into place in the Nave.

All sing:

THE NATIONAL ANTHEM

God save our gracious Queen,
Long live our noble Queen,
God save the Queen,
Send her victorious,
Happy and glorious,
Long to reign over us,
God save the Queen.

Thesaurus Musicus (c1743)
arranged by Gordon Jacob (1895-1984)

ORDER OF SERVICE

The Cortege, preceded by the Collegiate Body, moves to the Quire and Sacrarium, during which the Choir sings

THE SENTENCES

I am the resurrection and the life, saith the Lord: he that believeth in me, though he were dead, yet shall he live: and whosoever liveth and believeth in me shall never die.
(St John 11:25,26)

I know that my Redeemer liveth, and that he shall stand at the latter day upon the earth: and though after my skin worms destroy this body, yet in my flesh shall I see God; whom I shall see for myself, and mine eyes shall behold, and not another.
(Job 19: 25-27)

We brought nothing into this world, and it is certain we can carry nothing out. The Lord gave, and the Lord hath taken away; blessed be the name of the Lord.
(1 Timothy 6: 7; Job 1: 21)
William Croft (1678-1727)
Organist of Westminster Abbey (1708-27)

Thou knowest, Lord, the secrets of our hearts; shut not thy merciful ears unto our prayer; but spare us, Lord most holy, O God most mighty, O holy and most merciful Saviour, thou most worthy Judge eternal, suffer us not, at our last hour, for any pains of death, to fall from thee. Amen.
(Book of Common Prayer)
Henry Purcell (1659-95)
Organist of Westminster Abbey (1679-95)

I heard a voice from heaven, saying unto me, Write, From henceforth blessed are the dead which die in the Lord: even so saith the Spirit; for they rest from their labours.
(Revelations 14: 13) William Croft

*All remain standing. The Very Reverend
Dr Wesley Carr, Dean of Westminster, says*

THE BIDDING

We are gathered here in Westminster Abbey to give thanks for the life of Diana, Princess of Wales; to commend her soul to almighty God, and to seek his comfort for all who mourn. We particularly pray for God's restoring peace and loving presence with her children, the Princes William and Harry, and for all her family.

In her life, Diana profoundly influenced this nation and the world. Although a princess, she was someone for whom, from afar, we dared to feel affection, and by whom we were all intrigued. She kept company with kings and queens, with princes and presidents, but we especially remember her humane concerns and how she met individuals and made them feel significant. In her death she commands the sympathy of millions.

Whatever our beliefs and faith, let us with thanksgiving remember her life and enjoyment of it; let us rededicate to God the work of those many charities that she supported; let us commit ourselves anew to caring for others; and let us offer to him and for his service our own mortality and vulnerability.

Do not stand at my grave and weep.

I am not there, I do not sleep.

I am a thousand winds that blow,

I am the diamond glints on snow.

I am the sunlight on ripened grain,

I am the gentle autumn rain.

When you awaken in the morning's hush

I am the swift uplifting rush

of quiet birds in circled flight.

I am the soft stars that shine at night.

Do not stand at my grave and cry.

I am not there, I did not die.

ANON

All remain standing to sing

THE HYMN

I vow to thee, my country,
all earthly things above,
entire and whole and perfect,
the service of my love:
the love that asks no question,
the love that stands the test,
that lays upon the altar
the dearest and the best;
the love that never falters,
the love that pays the price,
the love that makes undaunted
the final sacrifice.

And there's another country,
I've heard of long ago,
most dear to them that love her,
most great to them that know;
we may not count her armies,
we may not see her King;
her fortress is a faithful heart,
her pride is suffering;
and soul by soul and silently
her shining bounds increase,
and her ways are ways of gentleness
and all her paths are peace.

Cecil Spring-Rice (1859-1918)
Gustav Holst (1874-1934)

I am the same age as the Queen and I feel like I have lost a daughter. I have never seen anything like this. And I know I never will again. I have never seen so many people all together in one place in my whole life. And I have never seen so many people crying, so many flowers, such an outpouring of grief. She was a natural, a gift from God. I have always had a great respect for the Royal family but it was Diana who caught my imagination. She was so full of compassion, so full of love for everyone regardless of race or creed. She reached out to everyone and won all our hearts. It's been a grand send-off for a great lady.

All sit.
Lady Sarah McCorquodale reads:

If I should die and leave you here awhile,
Be not like others, sore undone, who keep
Long vigils by the silent dust, and weep.
For my sake – turn again to life and smile,
Nerving thy heart and trembling hand to do
Something to comfort other hearts than thine.
Complete those dear unfinished tasks of mine
And I, perchance, may therein comfort you.

A. Price Hughes

All remain seated.

I have not been able to stop crying since I heard the news. I can't believe she has gone.

*If tears could build
a stairway,
And memories a lane.
I'd walk right up to heaven
And bring you back again.*

*The BBC Singers, together with Lynne Dawson,
Soprano, sing:*

Libera me, Domine, de morte aeterna,
in die illa tremenda quando coeli
movendi sunt, et terra:
dum veneris judicare saeculum per ignem.
Tremens factus sum ego et timeo, dum discussio
venerit, atque ventura ira.
Dies illa, dies irae, calamitatis et miseriae, dies
magna et amara valde.
Requiem aeternam dona eis Domine, et lux
perpetua luceat eis.

Deliver me, O Lord, from eternal death in
that dread day when the heavens and the
earth shall be shaken, and you will come to judge the
world by fire. I tremble in awe of the judgement and
the coming wrath. Day of wrath, day of calamity and
woe, great and exceeding bitter day. Rest eternal
grant unto them, O Lord, and let perpetual light
shine upon them.

*Giuseppe Verdi (1813-1901)
from The Requiem*

I found it quite difficult not to cry when William and
Harry walked by.

❦

They are grieving for their mum in front of you and
I found that very moving.

*All remain seated.
Lady Jane Fellowes reads:*

Time is too slow for those who wait,
too swift for those who fear,
too long for those who grieve,
too short for those who rejoice,
but for those who love, time is eternity.

Anon

With her tragic death a beacon of light has
been extinguished. Her good works brought hope to
so many of those in need throughout the world.

BARONESS THATCHER, FORMER PRIME MINISTER

She was an amazing woman, a real crusader who did
a great deal for others, and a loyal friend.

JEMIMA KHAN

All stand to sing

THE HYMN

The King of love my Shepherd is,
whose goodness faileth never;
I nothing lack if I am his
and he is mine forever.

Where streams of living water flow
my ransomed soul he leadeth,
and where the verdant pastures grow
with food celestial feedeth.

Perverse and foolish oft I strayed,
but yet in love he sought me,
and on his shoulder gently laid
and home rejoicing brought me.

In death's dark vale I fear no ill
with thee, dear Lord, beside me;
thy rod and staff my comfort still,
thy cross before to guide me.

Thou spread'st a table in my sight;
thy unction grace bestoweth:
and O what transport of delight
from thy pure chalice floweth!

And so through all the length of days
thy goodness faileth never:
good Shepherd, may I sing thy praise
within thy house for ever.

*Dominus regit me Psalm 23
J. B. Dykes (1823-76) and H. W. Baker (1821-77)*

All sit.
The Right Honourable Tony Blair, MP,
Prime Minister, reads

1 Corinthians 13

Though I speak with the tongues of men and of angels, and have not love, I am become as sounding brass, or a tinkling cymbal. And though I have the gift of prophecy, and understand all mysteries, and all knowledge; and though I have all faith, so that I could remove mountains, and have not love, I am nothing. And though I bestow all my goods to the poor, and though I give my body to be burned, and have not love, it profiteth me nothing.

Love suffereth long, and is kind; love envieth not; love vaunteth not itself, is not puffed up, doth not behave itself unseemly, seeketh not her own, is not easily provoked, thinketh no evil; rejoiceth not in iniquity, but rejoiceth in the truth; beareth all things, believeth all things, hopeth all things, endureth all things.

Love never faileth: but whether there be prophecies, they shall fail; whether there be tongues, they shall cease; whether there be knowledge, it shall vanish away. For we know in part, and we prophesy in part. But when that which is perfect is come, then that which is in part shall be done away.

When I was a child, I spake as a child, I understood as a child, I thought as a child: but when I became a man, I put away childish things. For now we see through a glass, darkly; but then face to face: now I know in part; but then shall I know even as also I am known. And now abideth faith, hope, love, these three; but the greatest of these is love.

The crowds are simply astonishing. But it doesn't surprise me – Diana was loved by millions of people in this country.

David Dimbleby,
BBC Broadcaster

I have, regretfully, been to a number of important State funerals at the Abbey, but this one had a warmth about it which is often missing at memorial services. Throughout the great length of the Abbey, there was a real sense of unity and affection for the Princess.

Lord Callaghan, Former Prime Minister

All remain seated.
Elton John sings:

CANDLE IN THE WIND

Bernie Taupin (b 1950) and Elton John (b 1947)

*Elton John's new version of Candle in the Wind became an immediate
number one chart hit, selling millions of copies around the world.
All royalties and profits from sales of the single are being donated to
the Diana, Princess of Wales Memorial Fund.*

I stand before you today the representative of a family in grief, in a country in mourning, before a world in shock. We are all united, not only in our desire to pay our respects to Diana, but rather in our need to do so.

For such was her extraordinary appeal that the tens of millions of people taking part in this service all over the world via television and radio, who never actually met her, feel that they too lost someone close to them in the early hours of Sunday morning.

It is a more remarkable tribute to Diana than I can ever hope to offer her today.

Diana was the very essence of compassion, of duty, of style, of beauty. All over the world she was a symbol of selfless humanity. All over the world, a standard bearer for the rights of the truly downtrodden, a very British girl who transcended nationality. Someone with a natural nobility who was classless and who proved in the last year that she needed no royal title to continue to generate her particular brand of magic. Today is our chance to say thank you for the way you brightened our lives, even though God granted you but half a life. We will all feel cheated, always, that you were taken from us so young and yet we must learn to be grateful that you came along at all.

Only now that you are gone, do we truly appreciate what we are now without, and we want you to know that life without you is very, very difficult.

We have all despaired at our loss over the past week, and only the strength of the message you gave us through your years of giving has afforded us the strength to move forward.

There is a temptation to rush to canonise your memory. There is no need to do so. You stand tall enough as a human being of unique qualities not to need to be seen as a saint. Indeed, to sanctify your memory would be to miss out on the very core of your being, your wonderfully mischievous sense of humour with a laugh that bent you double.

Your joy for life, transmitted wherever you took your smile and the sparkle in those unforgettable eyes; your boundless energy which you could barely contain.

But your greatest gift was your intuition and it was a gift you used wisely. This is what underpinned all your other wonderful attributes, and if we look to analyse what it was about you that had wide appeal, we find it in your instinctive feel for what was really important in all our lives.

Without your God-given sensitivity we would be immersed in greater ignorance at the anguish of AIDS and HIV sufferers, the plight of the homeless, the isolation of lepers, the random destruction of landmines.

Diana explained to me once that it was her innermost feelings of suffering that made it possible for her to connect with her constituency of the rejected.

And here we come to another truth about her. For all the status, the glamour, the applause, Diana remained throughout a very insecure person at heart, almost childlike in her desire to do good for others so she could release herself from deep feelings of unworthiness, of which her eating disorders were merely a symptom. The world sensed this part of her character and cherished her for her vulnerability whilst admiring her for her honesty.

The last time I saw Diana was on July 1, her birthday, in London, when, typically, she was not taking time to celebrate her special day with friends but was guest of honour at a special charity fund-raising evening.

She sparkled, of course, but I would rather cherish the days I spent with her in March when she came to visit me and my children in our home in South Africa.

I am proud of the fact that, apart from when she was on display meeting President Mandela, we managed to contrive to stop the ever-present paparazzi from getting a single picture of her — that meant a lot to her.

These were days I will always treasure.

It was as if we had been transported back to our childhood when we spent such an enormous amount of time together – the two youngest in the family.

Fundamentally, she had not changed at all from the big sister who mothered me as a baby, fought with me at school and endured those long train journeys between our parents' homes with me at weekends. It is a tribute to her level-headedness and strength that despite the most bizarre-like life imaginable after her childhood, she remained intact, true to herself.

There is no doubt that she was looking for a new direction in her life at this time. She talked endlessly of getting away from England, mainly because of the treatment that she received at the hands of the newspapers. I don't think she ever understood why her genuinely good intentions were sneered at by the media, why there appeared to be a permanent quest on their behalf to bring her down. It is baffling.

My own and only explanation is that genuine goodness is threatening to those at the opposite end of the moral spectrum. It is a point to remember that of all the ironies about Diana, perhaps the greatest was this – a girl given the name of the ancient goddess of hunting was, in the end, the most hunted person of the modern age.

She would want us today to pledge ourselves to protecting her beloved boys, William and Harry, from a similar fate and I do this here Diana on your behalf.

We will not allow them to suffer the anguish that used regularly to drive you to tearful despair. And beyond that, on behalf of your mother and sisters, I pledge that we, your blood family, will do all we can to continue the imaginative way in which you were steering these two exceptional young men, so that their souls are not simply immersed by duty and tradition, but can sing openly as you planned.

We fully respect the heritage into which they have both been born and will always respect and encourage them in their royal role, but we, like you, recognise the need for them to experience as many different aspects of life as possible to arm them spiritually and emotionally for the years ahead. I know you would have expected nothing less from us.

William and Harry, we all care desperately for you today. We are all chewed up with the sadness at the loss of a woman who was not even our mother. How great your suffering is, we cannot even imagine.

I would like to end by thanking God for the small mercies He has shown us at this dreadful time. For taking Diana at her most beautiful and radiant and when she had joy in her private life.

Above all, we give thanks for the life of a woman I am so proud to be able to call my sister, the unique, the complex, the extraordinary and irreplaceable Diana, whose beauty, both internal and external, will never be extinguished from our minds.

My feelings about The Earl Spencer's Tribute to his Sister

_____

_____

_____

_____

_____

_____

_____

All stand to sing

THE HYMN

Make me a channel of your peace:
where there is hatred let me bring your love,
where there is injury, your pardon, Lord,
and where there's doubt, true faith in you:

O Master grant that I may never seek
so much to be consoled as to console;
to be understood as to understand,
to be loved, as to love with all my soul!

Make me a channel of your peace:
where there's despair in life let me bring hope,
where there is darkness, only light,
and where there's sadness, ever joy:

O Master grant that I may never seek
so much to be consoled as to console;
to be understood as to understand,
to be loved, as to love with all my soul!

Make me a channel of your peace:
it is in pardoning that we are pardoned,
in giving of ourselves that we receive,
and in dying that we're born to eternal life.

O Master grant that I may never seek
so much to be consoled as to console;
to be understood as to understand,
to be loved, as to love with all my soul!

Make me a channel of your peace:
where there is hatred let me bring your love,
where there is injury, your pardon, Lord,
and where there's doubt, true faith in you.

St Francis of Assisi
translated by Sebastian Temple

I felt that the Abbey seemed not so much a place of worship, but a focal point for millions of people both at home and abroad to be able to express their grief.

LORD DEEDES, JOURNALIST AND AUTHOR

My deepest sympathy goes out to all the Royal Family and particularly to her two sons, to whom she was devoted.

CARDINAL BASIL HUME

All sit.
The Most Reverend and Right Honourable Dr George Carey, Lord Archbishop of Canterbury, Primate of All England and Metropolitan, leads

THE PRAYERS

For Diana, Princess of Wales

We give thanks to God for Diana, Princess of Wales; for her sense of joy and for the way she gave so much to so many people.

Lord, we thank you for Diana, whose life touched us all and for all those memories of her that we treasure. We give thanks for those qualities and strengths that endeared her to us; for her vulnerability; for her radiant and vibrant personality; for her ability to communicate warmth and compassion; for her ringing laugh; and above all for her readiness to identify with those less fortunate in our nation and the world.

Lord of the loving: **hear our prayer.**

For her family

We pray for those most closely affected by her death: for Prince William and Prince Harry who mourn the passing of their dearly loved mother; for her family, especially for her mother, her brother and her sisters.

Lord, we thank you for the precious gift of family life, for all human relationships and for the strength we draw from one another. Have compassion on those for whom this parting brings particular pain and the deepest sense of loss. Casting their cares on you, may they know the gentleness of your presence and the consolation of your love.

Lord of the bereaved: **hear our prayer.**

For the Royal Family

We pray for the Members of the Royal Family, for wisdom and discernment as they discharge their responsibilities in the United Kingdom, the Commonwealth and the world.

Lord, we commend to you Elizabeth our Queen, the Members of the Royal Family and all who exercise power and authority in our nation. Enrich them with your grace, that we may be governed with wisdom and godliness: so that in love for you and service to each other we may each bring our gifts to serve the common good.

Lord of the nations: **hear our prayer.**

For all who mourn

Diana was not alone in losing her young life tragically. We remember too her friend, Dodi al-Fayed and his family; Henri Paul, and all for whom today's service rekindles memories of grief untimely borne.

Lord, in certain hope of the resurrection to eternal life, we commend to you all who have lost loved ones in tragic circumstances. Give them comfort; renew their faith and strengthen them in the weeks and months ahead.

Lord of the broken-hearted: **hear our prayer.**

For the Princess's life and work

The Princess will be especially missed by the many charities with which she identified herself. We recall those precious images: the affectionate cuddle of children in hospital; that touch of the young man dying of AIDS; her compassion for those maimed through the evil of land mines – and many more.

Lord, we pray for all who are weak, poor and powerless in this country and throughout the world; the sick, among them Trevor Rees-Jones; the maimed and all whose lives are damaged. We thank you for the way that Diana became a beacon of hope and a source of strength for so many. We commend to you all those charities that she supported. Strengthen the resolve of those who work for them to continue the good work begun with her.

Lord of the suffering: **hear our prayer.**

For ourselves

And now abide faith, hope, love, these three; but the greatest of these is love. As we reflect on the Princess's compassion for others, we pray that we too may be inspired to serve as she served.

Lord, we thank you for Diana's commitment to others. Give us the same compassion and commitment. Give us a steadfast heart, which no unworthy thought can drag down; an unconquered heart, which no tribulation can wear out; an upright heart, which no unworthy purpose can tempt aside. Grant us, O Lord, understanding to know you, diligence to seek you, wisdom to find you, and a faithfulness that may bring us to your eternal kingdom.

Lord of the compassionate: **hear our prayer.**

She was an inspiration the world over that went beyond fashion, working for so many important causes, making her more than a style icon. On a personal level, she had a gorgeous sense of irony and was always one of the girls.

JOHN GALLIANO

I thank God for the gift of Diana and for all her loving and giving. I give her back to Him with my love, pride and admiration to rest in peace.

FRANCES SHAND KYDD, DIANA'S MOTHER

This world has very few people like Diana, who work so devotedly for the well-being of the poor, deprived and down-trodden people.

IMRAN KHAN

She did everything from the heart. Her heart ruled her head, which is why, I think, she was so often misunderstood. As a friend she was steadfast and loyal, and whenever I had any setback in my life she was immediately there and would drop everything.

ROSA MONCKTON, DIANA'S CLOSE FRIEND

All remain seated.
The Choristers sing:

I would be true, for there are those that trust me.
I would be pure, for there are those that care.
I would be strong, for there is much to suffer.
I would be brave, for there is much to dare.
I would be friend of all, the foe, the friendless.
I would be giving, and forget the gift,
I would be humble, for I know my weakness,
I would look up, laugh, love and live.

Air from County Derry in G. Petrie:
The Ancient Music of Ireland (1853)
Howard Arnold Walter

There are no words strong enough to describe the pain. The world has lost the most compassionate of humanitarians and someone so special, whose presence can never be replaced.

THE DUCHESS OF YORK

The Archbishop continues:

Therefore, confident in the love and mercy of God, holding a living faith in God's mighty resurrection power, we, the congregation here, those in the streets outside and the millions around the world, join one another and the hosts of heaven, as we say together, in whatever language we may choose, the prayer which Jesus taught us:

Our Father, who art in heaven,
hallowed be thy Name.
Thy kingdom come,
thy will be done,
on earth as it is in heaven.
Give us this day our daily bread.
And forgive us our trespasses,
as we forgive those who trespass against us.
And lead us not into temptation,
but deliver us from evil:
For thine is the kingdom, the power,
and the glory, for ever and ever. Amen.

This was not an occasion for military pomp. She was the People's Princess. . . I'm thrilled that there was such a big audience around the world. Rather like JFK, Diana meant so much to so many people in every continent.

LORD ATTENBOROUGH, FILM MAKER

The Archbishop says:

THE BLESSING

The God of peace who brought again from
the dead our Lord Jesus, that great shepherd
of the sheep, make you perfect in every good work to
do his will: and the blessing of God almighty, the
Father, the Son, and the Holy Spirit, be with you
and all whom you love, this day and for evermore.
Amen.

All stand to sing

THE HYMN

Guide me, O thou great Redeemer,
pilgrim through this barren land;
I am weak, but thou art mighty,
hold me with thy powerful hand:
bread of heaven,
feed me now and evermore.

Open now the crystal fountain
whence the healing stream doth flow;
let the fiery cloudy pillar
lead me all my journey through:
strong deliverer,
be thou still my strength and shield.

When I tread the verge of Jordan,
bid my anxious fears subside;
death of death, and hell's destruction,
land me safe on Canaan's side:
songs and praises
I will ever give to thee.

Cwm Rhondda W. Williams (1717-91)
John Hughes (1873-1932)
translated by P. Williams (1727-96), and others

Diana had a capacity for love and a willingness to go
anywhere to help anyone in need. That is something that will
always be remembered, and earned her admirers in every
corner of the globe. I will always remember Diana for her
tremendous sense of fun and her wonderful gift
of friendship.

**DIANA'S STEPMOTHER, RAINE SPENCER,
COMTESSE DE CHAMBRUN**

It really hit me when the Earl started talking personally about
her and her insecurities. That was when I wept, because that
was the person I knew for 14 years.

WAYNE SLEEP, DANCER

Standing before the Catafalque, the Dean says

The Commendation

Let us commend our sister Diana to the mercy of
God, our Maker and Redeemer.

Diana, our companion in faith and sister
in Christ, we entrust you to God.
Go forth from this world in the love of the Father,
who created you;
In the mercy of Jesus Christ, who died for you;
In the power of the Holy Spirit,
who strengthens you.
At one with all the faithful, living and departed,
may you rest in peace and rise in glory,
where grief and misery are banished
and light and joy evermore abide. Amen.

All remain standing as the Cortege leaves the church,
during which the Choir sings:

Alleluia. May flights of angels
sing thee to thy rest.
Remember me O Lord, when you
come into your kingdom.
Give rest O Lord to your handmaid,
who has fallen asleep.
The choir of saints have found the
well-spring of life, and door of paradise.
Life: a shadow and a dream.
Weeping at the grave creates the song:
Alleluia. Come, enjoy rewards and crowns
I have prepared for you.

John Tavener (b 1944)
extracts from William Shakespeare: Hamlet *and the*
Orthodox Funeral Service

At the west end of the church the Cortege halts for the
minute's silence, observed by the Nation.

The half-muffled bells of the Abbey church are rung.

All remain standing as the Processions move
to the west end of the church.

Music after the service:
Prelude in C minor, BWV546
Johann Sebastian Bach
Maestoso, from Symphonie no. 3
Camille Saint-Saens (1835-1921)

Members of the Congregation are requested
to remain in their places until invited by the
stewards to move.

She seized the imagination of young and old alike.
This beautiful woman was also a very vulnerable human
being, and out of that came lots of strength, her passion
and her commitment to people.
The world has lost a vibrant, lovely young person.
The word passion seems to sum her up – commitment
to issues, to causes.

George Carey, Archbishop of Canterbury

My own thoughts for Diana

Going Home on a Wave of Love

After leaving Westminster Abbey, the pall bearers carefully placed Diana's coffin into a hearse for the journey to her family home at Althorp, Northamptonshire. The crowds broke into spontaneous applause as the earlier tension and silence gave way to the adoration that the Princess had enjoyed in life. Flowers were strewn in front of the moving cortège and thrown on to the hearse, creating, as it were, a people's wreath. Slowly the hearse snaked through the London crowds to reach the motorway where every bridge was crowded with people wanting to say their final farewell.

By mid-afternoon the coffin reached Althorp where yet more mourners lined the route. Another mountain of flowers flanked the gates of Althorp estate and Diana's coffin disappeared from public view for the last time. Diana was home. Now was the time for her family to mourn privately and lay her to rest peacefully on an island set in a lake. In this beautifully tranquil place Diana can rest, assured that the world is a better place simply through her grace and kindness.

The quiet was just unearthly as we
walked through the crowds to get here.
That is something I'll never forget,
above everything else that's happened.

※

What she has done will live on and
being here today is like being part
of history.

※

You brought so much joy into the lives
of so many people.
You will be sadly missed but
you will always be our
Queen of Hearts.

Death is nothing at all.
I have only slipped away into the next room.
I am I, and you are you.
Whatever we were to each other, we are still.
Call me by my old familiar name, speak to me in the easy way
which you always used.
Put no difference into your tone, wear no forced air of solemnity,
or sorrow.
Laugh as we always laughed — at the little jokes we
enjoyed together.
Play, smile, think of me, pray for me.
Let my name be ever the household word that it
always was.
Let it be spoken without effort, without the ghost of
a shadow on it.
Life means all that it ever meant.
It is the same as it ever was, there is absolute
and unbroken continuity.
What is this death, but a negligible accident?
I am but round the corner.
All is well.

CANON SCOTT HOLLAND, FROM A SERMON PREACHED AT
ST PAUL'S CATHEDRAL IN 1910

Life is mostly froth and bubble,
Two things stand like stone:
Kindness in another's trouble,
Courage in your own.

ADAM LINDSAY GORDON, 19TH-CENTURY AUSTRALIAN POET.
QUOTED BY PRINCESS DIANA AT A BREAST CANCER FUND-
RAISING EVENT IN WASHINGTON D.C. IN SEPTEMBER 1996.

It is sad that you had to die for us to realise how much you were loved.

Thank you for your love and compassion and dedication to all people.

You are safe now, my little angel.

A person is not judged by how much they love, but by how much others love them, be happy.

Diana, the whole world loved you. You were the best and will never be forgotten. God bless you.

Diana, thank you for being the brightest star, I want you to have my wedding bouquet (I was married yesterday). You will never be forgotten.

Diana, I miss you. Thank you for being my Princess.

You never know what you've got until it's too late. I never knew her death would hit me so strongly. It's like the death of a best friend.

We are still in a deep shock. The tears have yet to flow. But when they come we don't know how we will ever stop them.

Such a vibrant life cut short.

I'm not a royal fan but Diana was amazing and she had a real common touch that appealed to so many people.

Diana was the most wonderful person. It's an enormous privilege to have known her, she will always be in our thoughts and hearts

There has been so much grief over her death. Now it's time to celebrate her life and the way she touched the people, especially those who were suffering.

We all loved her so much. The number of people paying their respects shows what an amazing role she played as part of our nation.

Diana will be greatly missed, she was everybody's light in their hours of darkness. Now let us be hers and pray that she will keep the world in her arms. The work she has done will continue, knowing she is forever looking down spreading her love.

Prayer for a Princess

Lord we thank you for the gift of Diana
For her readiness to show love; to hug and to touch
For the new hope she brought into so many sad lives
For the inspiration she gave to the nation;
that she gave to the world.
Gather her, Lord, into your loving arms
Be with William and Harry in their great loss.
Help us to grieve but not gape, to pray but not pry.
May the memory of her life and the sure hope of a greater
life to come make us the better men and women
in our work and in our lives.
In your name, we ask it.
Amen.

CANON JOHN OATES,
RECTOR OF ST BRIDE'S CHURCH, FLEET STREET

Diana, eventually the flowers will wither and die.
Your memory never will.

Our children's
children will hear
of you!
May you rest in
peace Diana.

Guardian angels at thy bed, sleep peaceful
lovely princess.

❧

The sleepy angels within awoke,
A beautiful lady unto them spoke:
'Give them love, peace and hope
And with the wind in their face
The strength and courage to take my place'.

❧

The brightest flames always burn for the shortest
time. She taught us how to care for others even
when we had despair of our own.
We love you Diana and will miss you.

Diana, never again will
the world know and love
another like you.

❧

Princess Diana,
wonderful lady, good and
kind. Lovely memories
you left behind.

❧

Diana and Dodi,
together forever. Our
love is with you always.

❧

Thank you for bringing
heaven and earth
closer together.

Princes William and Harry, the nation shares
your sorrow. Although we didn't know
Diana like you did, we will miss her deeply.
Don't ever forget the values she taught you in
life. If there were more people like her, the
world would be a better place.

I will arise and go now, for always night and day
I hear lake water lapping with low sounds by the shore;
While I stand on the roadway, or on the pavements gray,
I hear it in the deep heart's core.

W.B. YEATS, THE LAKE ISLE OF INNISFREE

Gone from us but not forgotten,
Never will our memories fade,
Sweetest thoughts shall
ever linger,
Round the spot where she
is laid.

You always had a smile
to share,
Time to give and time to care.
A loving nature kind and true,
These are the memories
I have of you.

She sleeps now in this sweet earth
This Emerald Isle
The extraordinary Lady Compassion
Diana, the Princess of Wales!
Such ample measure she gave of her womanhood
Of her Royal status to the good causes everywhere
Such eager virtue she gave to natural law
In more than natural love who raised the base
In man to better than itself.

Oh fragrant grave, Oh well worn rest!
Oh God who made this garden
This Isle for her to rest
How shall she rest?
Whose lightest thought was swift to serve the meek
The sick and the weak,
And the establishment, too?
Whose soul and mind were wings for the dove
Of Peace and Love.

The brightest star will
now be shining in the
midnight sky.

Diana, rose of England,
a wonderful mother,
rest in peace.

You will always be in our
thoughts and prayers.

Diana's Legacy

Tragically Diana has been taken from us, but her legend will live on forever. From the tiniest village to the largest city across the world, heart-stirring messages of love have been collected and sent to her family. Drawings and mementoes from children will be cherished because it was the young who stole her heart. It was as if we all knew her personally and shared a part of her very public life.

She was a role model for today's woman, proving that being glamorous need not mean failing to understand the harsher realities of life. Diana knew only too well how difficult it was to find true happiness and even in the most trying times she never once forgot her people: those who were suffering, those who needed a helping hand. Diana was a shining example to many – as caring mother or compassionate crusader. The comforting messages sent to her sons indicate that her people will always be there for them, as Diana would have wished.

Diana was a true woman of the Nineties. She took control of her life and showed she wasn't going to be manipulated by any situation that came her way.
She had the inner strength of a hundred men. She gave every woman who could relate to her the same strength too.

She was one in a million who helped a lot of people.

We will always remember Diana as the patron saint of children and people in need everywhere.

❦

Diana, our beautiful people's Princess, will live forever in our hearts.

*Diana practised her philosophy: to make
random acts of kindness every day.*

Queen of Hearts,
mother, campaigner,
listener, friend, sleep in
peace, Goodbye.

Diana, beautiful in mind,
body, soul and spirit.
God bless you.

A beautiful rose
chosen for God's garden.
God bless, sweet
Princess Diana.

A cluster of beautiful
memories, sprayed with a
million tears. Goodbye.

Time passes, memories
stay. Diana you will be
loved and remembered
every day.

My last goodbye to Diana

*Among the hidden minefields
Beneath a southern sky,
She hugged the crippled children
And heard their mothers' cry.
Who else among our leaders
could do this simple thing,
To help another human
And make the
angels sing?*

Diana touched
our hearts in such
a special way, the
world will never
know another woman
of such kindness
and wonder.

Our Personal Tributes
to Princess Diana

*T*his special book is for your family to cherish, and on these pages you may wish to record your feelings and memories of the Princess and treasure them forever.

_____

_____

_____

_____

_____

_____

_____

_____

_____

_____

_____

_____

_____

_____

_____

_____